Praise for *TAKING TO WATER*

"The flathead fish—whose sex can be difficult to determine until maturity, which can take years—is a recurring image in *Taking to Water*. Jennifer Conlon juxtaposes this with human society's insistence on assigning sex (and gender, accordingly) to children at birth, as the poems in this arresting book argue for an alternative:

>   if not *boys & girls*
> then alive   without classification
> alive   against form

The urgency here is as much about sex and gender as about the trauma, violence, and violation that, by ignoring them, society (parents, teachers, the church) condones, depending on the assumptions made about a person's sex and gender. In poems of masterful precision and relentless interrogation past the surface of identity into identity's beautiful complexity, Conlon asks 'what does it mean to control your own body to con- / tort your own sweetness.' 'My gender,' they argue, 'is a war between layers,' going on to say that if rainbow means a spectrum of color, gender is a 'dispersion of a body / of light.' *Taking to Water* is a startling, necessary collection; what Conlon says about gender's spectrum can also be said for this book: 'it will move across you do not be afraid.'"

—CARL PHILLIPS, author of *Then the War: And Selected Poems*

"If you aren't from the southeastern US, chances are good you've never heard of noodling. And even if you have heard of it, with a name like noodling, it would be easy to miss the skill, danger, and genuine collaborative attention it requires. Jennifer Conlon is an expert noodler of the patriarchal church, of family, of the gender binary—all of which is to say, misogynist systems of violence. Yet also with an eye on the world that 'loves them like flowers / mouthing their sun,' this poet is also expert at noodling the heart.

'I read hundreds of fish species / change from girl to boy / & back & forth like this.' Get wet with this water, friends. We are going from 'girl to boy, boy to girl, girlboy to gold to boygirl to girlgoldboy to boygoldgirl.'"

—TC TOLBERT, author of *Gephyromania* and co-editor of *Troubling the Line: Trans and Genderqueer Poetry and Poetics*

"Jennifer Conlon's *Taking to Water* is the most transformative collection of poems I've read. When Conlon's speaker says 'let there be life in me / in my own beginning' we are given a home in this affirmation of queer resilience, where self-fulfillment can stretch the landscape until the landscape agrees. *Taking to Water* captures the search for the ways the world could make room for us, 'make room / for my body & all / that comes with it.' Conlon has given us a sharper, better lyric to inhabit and demand the world with."

—C.T. SALAZAR, author of *Headless John the Baptist Hitchhiking*

TAKING TO WATER

TAKING TO WATER

JENNIFER CONLON

AUTUMN
HOUSE PRESS
Pittsburgh, PA

Cover Art by Kinsley Stocum
Book Design by Kinsley Stocum
Author Photo by Jennifer Conlon

LIBRARY OF CONGRESS CATALOGING-IN-PUBLICATION DATA
NAMES: Conlon, Jennifer, author.
TITLE: Taking to Water / Jennifer Conlon.
DESCRIPTION: Pittsburgh, PA : Autumn House Press, 2023
IDENTIFIERS: LCCN 2023016852 (print) | LCCN 2023016853 (ebook) |
    ISBN 9781637680766 (paperback) | ISBN 9781637680773 (epub)
SUBJECTS: LCGFT: Poetry.
CLASSIFICATION: LCC PS3603.O5416 T35 2023 (print) | LCC PS3603.O5416 (ebook) |
    DDC 811/.6--dc23/eng/20230609
LC record available at https://lccn.loc.gov/2023016852
LC ebook record available at https://lccn.loc.gov/2023016853

Printed in the United States on acid-free paper that meets the international standards of permanent books intended for purchase by libraries.

Autumn House Press is a nonprofit corporation whose mission is the publication and promotion of poetry and other fine literature. The press gratefully acknowledges support from individual donors, public and private foundations, and government agencies. This book was supported, in part, by the Greater Pittsburgh Arts Council through its Allegheny Arts Revival Grant and the Pennsylvania Council on the Arts, a state agency funded by the Commonwealth of Pennsylvania, and the National Endowment for the Arts. To find out more about how National Endowment for the Arts grants impact individuals and communities, visit www.arts.gov.

TABLE OF CONTENTS

▽

∇

TAKING TO WATER

TONGUES

every time I faked
speaking in tongues
I made a new god

sucked them
right on out the clay
lapped their mouth

out of my mouth
my sound a ground to pray on
a moan to survive with

my made-up language
a spread of handless wrists
wrestling   imagine

your god a word
what are they saying?
does it make your world hiss?

undo your vision?
if I make a new word for worship
my body heals   grows a new

scale or hair with the possibility
of making more
it can cover my whole damn body

with the word
do you think the god I make
could be a power   with no tongue?

BAIT

Momma's biggest concern
was me getting worms
from playing in dirt.

You could get so filled
with worms
they'd be up to your throat.

We'd have to sink you
in the pond
so the fish could deal with you.

The fish could empty me.
Empty beyond worms or dirt.
Wherever the body goes.
In the computer lab
I read hundreds of fish species
change from girl to boy
& back & forth like this
under the water
right next to the other fish
right there in light.

IN THE WILD

Men send scalers across fish sides.

I catch their shining flakes on newspaper under the gutting table.
When I have enough, I hide in the bathroom, press their sequins

to my body, practice lips in the mirror. Scales at my elbow form a fin.
A gill to cover my long neck. Mucus sticks the fish parts to my body.

I open & close my mouth, protrude my tongue. What does a fish do with its
tongue? Some fish have teeth on their tongue. Some fish have girl parasites

that eat the tongue & take its place. Her eyes will shrink, her legs stretch out
& she anchors herself in the mouth. The fish is minimally damaged.

When the fish dies, the girl parasite leaves the mouth,
clings to the head or body. No one knows

what happens next.

TAKING TO WATER

1.

Two days before third grade I hear them arguing about the bus. I ride the bus, but Momma says *not no more*. Dad Figure 2 says *bad things are always happening.*

2.

Brother asks *what does a dead girl in the river have to do with me? She didn't ride my bus or even go to my school.*

3.

The first day she drives me to school, I'm late. I cry. I'm too embarrassed to walk in. I know everyone will look at me, think I was too dumb to get here on time.

4.

Frogs live near water or else they will die if their skin dries out.

5.

In the lunchroom Stephanie splashes water on her face & pretends to be drowned at the table.

Britney says *that's not what it looks like.*

Alisha says *why are you making fun of a dead girl* so Stephanie stops, wipes the water off her face & eats her french fries.

6.

The name of a girl is.
The river was named by a

7.

At dinner I stare at fish sticks, wonder how her body got from a bus stop to the river. How many kids assigned *Girl* can this happen to? How many have skin that don't take to water?

8.

The common pond frog is ready to breed at only *three years old.*

Only:

         1. *without others or anything further*
         2. *alone, solely*
         3. *merely, just*
         4. *as recently as*
         5. *in the final outcome*

9.

I draw the outline of a girl. I draw it smooth & wet the skin. Her gills get her from the bus to the river alive. Fin spines make it hard to touch her there, especially if she's moving & she is.

10.

The school cancels our field trip to the river. Imagine seeing her bloated body receiving kisses from flies. Her skin a violence even in death, *only* she is probably still here. She must have just swam off.

ASSIGNED FEMALE AT BIRTH

There was the long
drive around the drowned bridge.

There was the birth.
Momma a position
in the hospital bed.

Dad Figure 1 said I wouldn't open
my sea-murky eyes until
the lights were out.

I wasn't ready
for the fluorescence
to assign me *Girl.*

Let me stay the dark until I can
create my own revolving
light.

Let me stay the dark form
questioning questioning
questioning . . .

HOW TO MEASURE PAIN FROM A PORCH-STEP

Dad Figure 2 is sleeping on the lawn
nose like morning dew candy—
a mass of hardened sugary knobs
melted & re-formed into the shape of the candy bowl.

His plump arms. A swirl of peach
& mud. Momma leaves him outside for the better
part of the afternoon, says *Don't mess with him.*
I sit on the porch-step. I watch his body leak,
a spring of sugar running from his nose,

pooling above his lip, attracting ants.
First three, then ninety-nine. I stop counting,
guess about four billion ants press on his body.

Do they weigh as much as he does, combined? Their mandibles
grace his skin, antennae flickering. How long will it take
for them to suck out his sugar? I start counting again.

AN ANIMAL GROWING

"Here is the secret: the end is an animal growing by accretion, image by image, vote by vote."
—Jorie Graham

Voracious carnivores, flathead catfish feed primarily on other fish, insects, annelid worms & crustaceans. Submerged logs, other debris form their nests. The male builds the nest & fans the clutch. The size of the clutch varies proportionally to the size of the female. An average of 2,640 eggs per kilogram of fish are laid. Young flatheads are cannibalistic & therefore cannot be used in fish farming.

▼

To eliminate any fishy taste, simply soak the catfish in milk for an hour before frying. Bread with seasoned cornmeal & fry filets in batches. The catfish are done when most of the bubbling stops & they begin to float.

▼

Dad Figure 2 drops the filet into cornmeal. The air is a flat sand. In the cornmeal-mist I can just make out the sharpness of his nose, a contrast to the rest of his pudgy body. How can he think about eating? Momma insisted he not let me watch, but I watched. I saw him drag our dog into the tree line & put the Magnum to her ear. When he came back to our sobs, he said *it's a bullet or a vet bill & I've got a bullet*. I bury her rock by rock as the fall comes.

▼

Although the concept of catching fish with only the use of an arm in the water is simple enough, the process of noodling is more complicated. The choice of catfish as prey is not arbitrary. Most noodlers have spotters who help them bring catfish in, either to shore or to their boat; noodling in pairs is considered important for safety. Noodling partners often form long-term partnerships.

▼

I cannot eat the fish. Dad Figure 2 says *You will eat it or you will go sit at the bottom of the pond.* There, I spot a carp munching pondgrass. He spits a pile into my lap. I eat & eat & eat.

▼

I think I am drowning but I can hear him laughing & Momma is also laughing so I must not be drowning but resisting the fun of it. *Stop kicking,* I can hear him say through seventeen miles of water. *The bitch hit me in the nuts.* Momma pulls me out of the water by my foot. *Watch what you do with those things. You could really hurt him.*

▼

The average punishment for rape is. The average punishment for molestation is. The average punishment for imprisonment is. The average punishment for. I'm probably making all of this up.

▼

To *avenge* is "to get revenge" or "to take vengeance." It suggests the administration of just punishment for an immoral act. *Revenge* seems to stress the idea of retaliation a bit more strongly & implies real hatred as its motivation.

▼

You would think that all catfish live in the deepest part of the water, but flatheads make their bed in the shallows of a river bend, wait under a layer of mud for the moving thing. The moving thing may be a crawdad. The moving thing may be a woodlouse. The moving thing may be a sunfish. The moving thing may be a finger finding the mouth of a flathead who consumes the hand. The whole hand pulled in, hooking on gills. They pull the flathead out of the water by its mouth, barbels flinching.

CAN I JUST ENJOY THE WATER?

who remembers   the unknown origin
of *boys & girls*   the first fish
appeared without   precursor
no jaw or gender   no parents or scales
oh two chambered   heart
binary lies   if not *boys & girls*
then alive   without classification
alive   against form

a bright appearance

                        there in the water

CONJURING THE CLOSET

Every time I say it aloud
the memory
conjures itself a brick.

It builds the house
& locks me
in the small
room of the east corner
one with no windows
a crawl space
ajar
doors that only lead to closets.

I rattle
the crystal doorknobs
stare
into their mirrors
multiplied.

CHURCH

I pray
Amen

I'm learnin
Amen

language the head
I pray a sound
I pray the river

If the brown water
nudges my ankles
let em sleep

If the water
percussion my calves
let me widen my legs
If the water pulls on my knees
let me fall on em
let the silt & mud
leak into wrinkles
let mud go on in

If the water
shocks my thighs
let there be therapy
let the water tell me
I am safe Amen

If the water
reaches my pussy lips

let em shimmer tickle
let em home the water Amen
ask for its direction

If the water
tastes my hip bones
let it suck em til
I moan Amen
let it suck like a rat snake
on a fresh chicken egg

If the water
perceives my belly fills
my belly button
let there be life in me
in my own beginning

If the water erases my rib
let all the men fall
down on muddy knees & thank us
for the opportunity of
wet pussy wet mind

If the water Amen
meets my breasts
let my nipples harden & smile

If the water joins
my breasts let it hold there
the water undulating breathing
up my sternum like the snake spine
wraps a branch
breathes the tree Amen

If the water constricts my breasts
let me inhale let me inhale
If the water holds me at my neck

let me tell you bitch
lemme tell you

about the effort of exhale
of sonic wave moving
through the body so fast
it breathes it breathes solid-toothed
& belly-grounded
like a copperhead outmovin
the shovel

If the water
gestures my mouth
let me open the estuary
envelope the river
every catfish named & unnamed
especially ones waitin under mud
every water strider & fallin helicopter
plant every bug I can't name yet
holdin onto a rock

kneeless Amen
sharp their eyes saying *breathe breathe*

If the water
bobs my temples up & down
let me pray Amen
let me return to the language
of river bend river bodied
through the rootwad of us

Fixed wet ankles
wait for the mud
water tangle the eyes

If the water
lifts my eyes Amen
let me see Amen
lemme see the flathead catfish lip
at the sunfish bottom mouth it
into a stone throat into a path like belly
like process
an arrival like a great big
string of fish shit
we are becoming

Fuck witness
Why are you watching me wet
watching this drown brown water
If the water Amen
tempts my temples again
bobbing & bobbing

Let me question this prayer
this question
this river is a way
to god not a prayer
but a body
of water Amen

If the body
coats my head
floats my hair
into the surface

let me better view Amen
lemme tree a reach Amen

pull myself up by the branch
ask a question of god
that assures them I'm here
believin in Amen
in the river & mud &

the flathead saying
fill your body & never go home

LAYERS

I dig into the river for my future.
Layers of sex long dead carapace.
Beetle tongue.

I dig until I hit the truth about mud.
My gender is a war between layers.
Fish bone on fish bone make my
gravestone.

HOUSE FIRE

Miss Jones leads us to the auditorium
where Firefighter Man stands
by a miniature wood house.

In this scenario my parent is Miss Jones
who dotes outside the window, insists
I not get discouraged as my house
burns me out of it.

A boy barges forward,
asks if we will get to see a firetruck today
& he is promised *yes.*

We are asked to pretend
the house is on fire & it's not hard
because they've painted believable flames
over the doors, licking up windows.

Firefighter Man shows *the boys & girls* how to test
orange-painted doorknobs for heat
& how to get from the bed to the window

alive with such small fingers.
Alive like the fire & the house & Miss Jones.
This house, like my grandma's, small
shelter for a wild animal & its descendants.

The doorway burns brilliant & bows to the weight
of the house. The house wants to live. It curls
& glows & holds me in its closet. Miss Jones

& Firefighter Man & barging boy all shouting
for me to get out. *Won't you join the other*
boys & girls? The boy is laughing at the flare
licking up my pink windbreaker pants.
Doesn't she know it's not real? It's a full house.

Everyone is watching me move like a planet
between rooms. The kitchen has its own imagination.
I shout back at barging boy *Of course it's real!*
Why do you think the firetrucks are here?

My grandma is in the kitchen pouring ginger ale
into a yellow sippy cup. She holds me
better than the closet, better than *boys & girls.*

Miss Jones's hand reaches in through the window,
her long manicured nails
catching flame like little matchsticks. How
could I ever save them?

GIRL, IF YOU DON'T CROSS YOUR LEGS

Select One

A) Ants will find your peach

B) You'll let all the faeries
out & what are you, *Girl,* without your faeries?

C) You'll be mistaken
for a cock warmer

D) You'll go to Hell with
all the other gaping girls

E) A man will hang a sign
from your thigh that says CUM DUMPSTER

F) The other girls will call
you Black Hole, Sperm Sucker, The Death of Adam,
Hot Pocket

G) All of the above & all at once

EIGHTH BIRTHDAY

Dad Figure 2
invites all his friends
orders a keg
hangs pink balloons for *Girl*

                    Momma balances
                    strawberry cake

                                        I am a small table

                    paper plates & cups
                    women's breasts
                    in red bikini tops

                                        Fried catfish floats
                                The coleslaw is a painting

Dad Figure 2 threatens
my jaw—

It might be your birthday
but you're going to eat,   *Girl.*

                                        I open the catfish
                                      I eat the breading
                                      I separate
                                      from the body

One of the men
congratulates
himself for *finely deboning*

this very fish
you're eatin,   *Girl.*

I gaze over at the fish
on their plates

But my fish doesn't look like theirs.

Mine has huge bones tremoring the plate, a gill
alarming, carries sorrow like a black egg.

DEAR THIGHS,

Can't you be trees?

Be loblolly pines
with scaly plates

bark that cannot smooth
no matter which direction
I'm stroked   fire resistant
windbreak   home
for Carolina chickadee
squirrel
wild turkey

Be fixed
in a river bottom

finger rip   river
breaks   every knuckle
        over your sweet armor

WHEN THERE IS NO EVIDENCE UPON INITIAL ASSESSMENT, WE MUST RE-EXAMINE THE BODY

1. Clothes are removed.

Visible injuries are documented,
measured & compared
to the gender of the clothes.
I am told these clothes are *Girl.*

2. The body is examined.

The scales
are raised by rubbing up the body
with the back of a knife.

An incision is made in the belly
button, carried
upward to the chin.

The guts & gills are removed,
roe if female—
these pull out easily.

Before separating the head, the mouth is examined.
What tongue lodges
in the throat? What shade of red begs the lips?

The presence of a tongue parasite indicates
possible femininity.

The inside of the body is rinsed with cold
running water until the water runs clear.
I am trying to run clear.

3. The body is discharged.

The skin is rinsed
if left on.

WITH OR WITHOUT SUNDAY CLOTHES, WE GO TO CHURCH

Momma's religious devotion was maintained by having a place to drop us
 kids on Wednesdays, Saturdays, Sundays & the whole summer.

The summer we got church assistance for camp, I let a man touch my fore-
 head. I pretended to talk in tongues. I fell down into older people's arms.

When the pastor took me in a back room to save me, he handed me a
 smelly used Bible with a pea-green cover, told me to write my name
 inside. Told me I'd be saved by the father.

I wondered if he knew. I wondered if he was a Dad Figure too.

FISHING WITH DAD FIGURE 2

I think about what it's like to suffocate
with eyes pressed to other eyes
as I pull the string of fish over the dock
into the cooler. The string slips out of gills
through my wetflesh palm. Fish rest
into one another's fluid gaze.

When the men form a line
to filet the fish, I watch them—
how they unzip the bellies.
Out comes the lake.

A couple of the men & Dad Figure 2
see me watching & watch back—
wait for me to unzip. I get mosquito bites
everywhere
just standing. Each of their eyes sucking
at my skin, looking for the spot
to push in.

ODE TO FLATHEAD CATFISH

in rootwads
water cloud, of log
& brush, collected
at bends
in rivers
your head, a shovel
your head, a spoon
sip of mercury
I want your
barbel, your pout
you mistaken eel
bony head sink
& grind
parts of you
are song, alarm
bell of flathead
earth tangle of timber
still, you wait
this deep pool
for sunfish, my finger
to come to your motion-
less mass sunk hard
as river rocks
You hear me in your bed
hear my body
the child of it, the bone
growin through
your blackwater
When you take my hand
I scoop your body up
belly

hammerin my thigh
your throat
a sheath
for my arm
spines
searching the sky
to stab, thrash
gulp & gulp
a sound
a man
speaking
through a plastic tube
He is asking a question
concerned with
size
you out of water
drunk, legend, lens
the least important
for men to fry
swindle into oil
absent
of drumming sounds
sweet earth
watch me
with your good eyes
say honeysuckle skin
say the only
predators
to flatheads
are flatheads
& us

HOW TO MEASURE PAIN FROM THE TOP OF AN OAK TREE

I leave my forest hideout to follow his scream,
hide behind an oak when I catch the sight of him—
Dad Figure 2 running circles around the stalled push-mower,

wasps in charge of his body.
He moves like Barney at a dance party. The wasps peck & peck
his cheeks, send red lip-prints up his knees, thighs,

above-thigh. I watch him unzip his pants.
Every last wasp freed. But they can taste his candy,
his fruit, blood of soda. The girl wasps push

their stinger into him over & over until he moans
on the grass-clippings a beautiful shade of blue,
his head like an ostrich-sized robin's egg. I climb

the oak for a better view just as Momma pulls
into the driveway. She fills her arms with groceries
before she spots the hardening blue whale in the yard.

From up here, I can count twenty-two stings.
If she'd just roll him over, I could count the rest.

WITCH HUNT

1.

In the shower I look
between my thighs.
My first stretch mark has appeared,
a pink bloody chasm.
Is this another opening
men will search for?
Another opening that signifies *Girl.*

2.

I take a box cutter to my thighs,
give the stretchmark the hope
of sameness, of seeing themself
outside of themself. I want to cut
deep enough.

I want to make the search myself,
see what is in there
that excites men to touch & hunt
for what overwhelms them,
see if I could
bleed it out.

3.

Here, blood coming out
of my *wherever.*

EIGHT WAYS OF MALE GAZE

1.

Five women surround a mudcat.
One fingers the hole,
slips her hand
into mouth.

2.

The largest flathead
left Kansas
a lover
of mottled mess,
has men kissing
pouts
as big as your two
hands &
two more.

3.

The taste,
a honeysuckle mound.
Fry-oil stings
the shovelhead.
Make it dance
alone in its bed.

4.

My first flatty
was released.
Dad Figure 1 slid it into the lake, said
the largest ones have mud in them.
He's been trying for four years
to get me off clay.

5.

I dream about a damp tangle
& wake up
in a yellow cat's skin.
My barbels
are a record
& everyone wants to kiss me.

6.

Once we mistook a flathead for an eel,
left it in the water,
an electric memory
like fork tines over a grave.

7.

All gods don't live
in the sea & if you don't believe
me, try drowning in the river
on a harvest moon
& see if a spoonbill
the size of your car
don't take your hand.

8.

Flatheads were made by a moose,
unmade by a man
with pipes as long
as the ocean
& as full
as history. He unmakes
the water.

MEN CAN'T SEE ME

after Elizabeth Bishop

If I'm under blackwater.
If I'm nestled in a pool. If I am scaled
reflective.
If my eyes are open.
If his rod is visible & he shakes it
loudly. If he knocks
his beer can into the water. If I remember
in this life not to bite the hook.
If I survive it's a trick of the worm.
If I steal the bait & leave him hollering
I'LL CATCH YOU GODDAMNIT.
If the other men encourage him.
If the other men also shout
CATCH THAT BITCH because they think
I'm a *Girl.*
If they know without seeing me.
If I already have six snagged lines hanging
from my mouth
like medals with their ribbons
frayed & wavering.
If I weigh too much.
If I can see moons through the water.
If my moans make the water move.
If my body moves without dimension.
If I change. If I'm not a *Girl.*
If scales bend light. If my lips. If I breathe
with my whole body.

WHEN YOU ARE THE FAMILY SECRET

First, sedate it. A small
amount of skullcap will do.
Make a wide incision behind
your tongue. Replace your tongue
with a tag that reads CONTROL.
There are various methods
for containing your secret.

One is the fireproof box
in the closet, where Momma places
the secret between
old weed & photos of her dead father.

You could share the secret over roasted chicken,
potatoes, wine. Announce the secret
as easy as buttered carrots.
Let the family eat the secret
so no one has to bring it up again.

Yet another method waives containment,
allows the subject to be a quiet bear
that peels you open like a picnic,
teething at your wicker sinews.
No one will hear the bear opening you.
No one will know you failed to sedate it.
Failed to cut the tongue. Failed
at making control look as easy as a word.

CHOOSE A PASSWORD: CHILDHOOD NICKNAME

Dad Figure 2 said *thunder thighs* as if
there was a storm between my legs,
thighs that make waves, divide the sky.

As if they weren't charged
with some force he couldn't see, the effort
of opening.

As if he could use the sound of me
to calculate the distance
between our bodies.

As if the speed of light is not
universal & my sound
will never catch up.

As if the god of Thursday didn't live
between my legs
with each of my steps.

As if the sound didn't shake him
from a deer stand or swimming pool,
make him jump out of the shower.

As if the presence of a thigh-gap
would allow him to see himself,
to imagine some space in me.

As if their size was relative
to his comfort, as if his comfort
could make a similar sound.

SOME FISH

Dad Figure 1 says our mouths are not like fish mouths
which may or may not have teeth.
He says the larger the mouth, the bigger
prey it can consume
& I reckon I can only consume gravel or
Momma's earrings or the sound
of Dad Figure 2 coming upstairs.

Some fish have teeth in the roof of their mouth.
Some fish have teeth in their throat
& I think I am one of these fish. I pull
everything I cannot hold
into my mouth like assorted sinkers
of various weights. My leathery throat

divides them there. Decides
what belongs deepest inside of me.
& there holds what does not belong
or has no permission to kiss or bait,
sink or pull, catch or gender,
to serve a family.

FATHER, SON

The pastor says I can't ask for *that* & God
has nothing to do with Dad Figures. What I pray
is an act of violence—   *Maybe if I was a boy.*
Pastor's God doesn't like this idea either.

         So I pray quiet for a new body:
         One with spine-coated thighs & skin that leaks
         poison. Mucus under my armpits.
         A swim bladder.   A swim bladder.

I pray for a new body for these men too. Hands
the size of a pecan
halved apart. Stomach
so bloated they can't reach through our doors.
Tender wings that melt in the water. Amen.

ESCAPE

row
of fish on a long table
longer than forever
I'll check
every fish lip
lifted for the girl
tongue parasite
I want to know
how she takes
to water
I want to see her
escape
the lip barrier
weeds nothing
in her way the lip
an escape of water
the row a possibility
a shape

HOME IS WHERE YOUR BODY LIVES

Dad Figure 2 kept the house
& we had to leave.
Kids at school asked why
I was riding the wrong
bus, wearing wrong clothes.

Ivy End, a brick
apartment with iron
window bars. My bedroom
ceiling dropped slow rain
the color of bluebells.

It took two weeks
to fill the pot. My job
was to empty it in the bathtub
& run back fast
enough to catch the next drop
& run back again to rinse
the tub before the stain set in.

& the kids asked if I missed
the house: the yard &
the pond & the fish fry's
& the big television. I said *no.*
I love my new home. I love it
because none of it is him
& he doesn't own every body
of water, every fish, every bloom.

I DREAM A GARDEN WHERE

I have killed off that *Girl*
I till
her body in

making sure no toes
are rising out of soil,
stretching like potato eyes.

I pour fire on my garden.
Her body wiggles like frying squash
in the clay, sucking at its wetness.

I wonder how alive she still is under there.
I let the fire soak the garden,

run my rake over her pale head,
see if the rest of her questioning
body will rise up.

There is nothing I can't grow here.

BAPTISTRY

The pastor drowns me in a plastic pool
with little cherubs on the lining
pushes my head into that foggy waterworld
of bobblehead Jesus & leftover demons
& deep-sea fish that glow
The cherubs smile into their hands
They are telling me *Come up come up*
Someone save this child

What gets saved with me
but the notion I'm a danger
What rescue in this body of mine
that you keep calling *Girl*
Hello boys & girls
Glow-fish states my peril
& floats me to the top
Floats me through the pool
& above families screaming
Floats me as far as original cloud
I come down when I'm dry
When I'm redeemed of all
their wasted water

ALTERNATIVE TO BURYING

A crow lies open
in the field,
three ants
moving atop
its breast.
The body has
communicated
death as sweetgrass,
as swerving air.
Soon the ants
will tell them all.
The crow a feather-
less need,
the memory
of unfolding
bone by tender splintering
bone.

HOW TO MEASURE PAIN FROM INSIDE A PACK OF RED WOLVES

The howling stars. Red wolves just inside
the tree line, noses poking into the moonlit yard.
They lift their heads. I left the fence gate open
just a sliver & now it's wide open. Red wolves
arouse the grass, shift their shoulders in slow motion
through our back door.   Each night,
they take something from him: a work tool,
eyebrow hairs, the gold watch, a strip of flesh from
a rough toe. Now a whole foot. Now a calf covered
in wiry fuzz. Now a hand. Now the other hand.
Now his tiny eyes, lids & all.

MY NEW MOTHER

the hummingbird misses its chance
i am an organ
of the earth the body
might jerk & shake
in its new home
my toes have grown since
i've last known them
we are all our own best mothers

my new mother does stretches
in the morning
lets me watch *Ren & Stimpy*
& eat Ben & Jerry's
right from the pint
my new mother is a bright
light on the porch moths
blazing dust in that halo of air
fireflies are the distance
each grass a flat thread for making

my future my new mother imagines
a college fund a faraway move
a classless struggle my new
mother makes the best cornbread
& succotash my new mother
listens to my body knows a poem
what a poem can undo in our body
my new mother doesn't care for
saints has already read the bible
but just for the poetry & irony

my new mother reads to me
books about revolution & queer joy
& my mother can imagine
new worlds   my mother is a new world
my new mother bought me periwinkle
roller skates & celebrates every turn
& shake & stop
my new mother rubs lavender eucalyptus
balm on my wrists temples feet
my new mother thinks i'll live a long
long time well past thirty-five well past
a pandemic my new mother
is the first person i came out to
my new mother has a genderfluid
child & loves them like flowers
mouthing their sun

SELF-GLOSSARY OF A GENDERFLUID KID

Alchemy: transformation of matter, as in iron to gold, gold to woman, girl to boy, boy to girl, girlboy to gold to boygirl to girlgoldboy to boygoldgirl

Body: I like sparkling water, flower baths, neck-kisses, homegrown tomatoes, sea stones

Closet: a purgatory, a dam, a drag show, a meditation chamber, pastor's Hell, collect yourself

Church: a purgatory, a dam, a drag show, a meditation chamber, pastor's Hell, collect yourself, tithe

Dad Figure: there is a statue   how did you imagine it?

Extinction: the risk of a body, the memory of a red wolf

Fish: not a thing that comes up for air

Faith: if you believe you are alive

Gender: _____ . . .

Home: deep deep deep deep deep deep inside of you   [it is you you you you]

I: you are determining you are you are you

Jaw: when I open you will know

Kudzu: what do you imagine protects you? Let it be.

Lake: a purse of water that holds all your living things

Men: performances of Dad Figures, available in matinee, dark night, or court-ordered every other weekend

New: body null body new body null body nobody null body new body null body nobody knew body

Oak: the first god I met & most I still meet, are trees

Parasite: I often dream of her there in the fish mouth guarding the entrance

Questioning: an act of faith in yourself, in the light if you wait for the sun to breach the hill

Red wolves: imagine your survival imagine it in red

River: imagine moving beyond your body imagine it wet

Spectrum: it will move across you do not be afraid

Tongue: an organ of chance, the mystery of river undulation may never be known to some

Unzip: to open or be opened by a force, usually after an audible or visible *Yes*

Vivisection: to be opened alive to watch the opening like a projector flashing on the ceiling for the rest of your life

Window: imagining wind

Witness: the lie that anyone watching will save you

X-ray: inside they find all the shredded license plates belonging to who I was before

Yard: count the bees, pluck the weeds, imagine you live in the forest

Zip: you are closing tight, dear. Let me see. *No.*

HOW TO MEASURE PAIN FROM A DREAM

He is wrapped in it. The kudzu is nearly entering him,
worming its way across his torso & shoulders until
Momma mistakes him for a tree in the yard, hangs
a birdfeeder from one limb. Birds shit on the tree.
Birds search the kudzu vines for fleshy bark

& when his body winces at their pinch,
the kudzu embraces him. He spoils: two heavy limbs,
drops of slow persimmons gathering in the kudzu litter.
We try to catch all of him, insert a tap to quicken the drip.

He fits into just two pails.

IN MY NEXT LIFE

I stand over
the fish, watch
their sun-warm
scales slide against
the ice, drawing
them smaller
one at a time.

After a couple
hours—the time
it takes the men
to drink the beer
fridge dry—
I can see them
swimming again.

I want to slide
in there with them,
between ice &
scales, make room
for my body & all
that comes with it.

SPECTRUM STUDY

I get it, I get it
rainbow: spectrum of color
gender: dispersion of a body
of light
I can't stop emitting
rays from pores
blue eyes everyone calls lake—
another spectrum of luminescence
grayscale the body
& you get a shadow diagram
my fin rays, my harp for a heart
what are breasts but one
or more carriers of light-cells—
blue & red coded forms
ripe in a windowsill
clavicle of bottomless shade
I am lucky for my body still
I turn away
from graphing the light
I am too unsure for lines
in dreams what splits me
but I can handle the color
the light pushing against my hips
birds turning through the cloud
dive for the empty mouth

TRANSFIGURING THE DINNER TABLE

i.

Bear massaging the ache of my neck,
claw pads redding the skin to life

i.

A red wolf in each chair, fingerbones
dangling their gums

i.

Gnats crowding my molasses mouth

i.

Wasps gather like braids
around the necks of turkey vultures,
thronging the blowhole of the blue whale

i.

A large flathead whole on a gold plate,
unbreaded & needless of water,
used to the air of me, our table round

enough that none of us call the edge
an end, but a slow falling under, a
genderfluid dreamscape

i.

Petrels form a line across my place mat,
feathery backs pressed
against my chest, waiting for mosquitos
to come

i.

Not one will make it to my flesh

WHORIGIN STORY

She said it was a tea stain
so many times my memory became
tea stain
Don't mommas know the truth

A tea stain is not a rape stain
not filled with myth blood openings

If it's tea I never bellyache it
never suture never stargaze
never pads filled black never
wonder if I found it could I
put it back

Tell me about the first time you became
a whore
without ever saying yes

My tea stain in the shape of
a must a might a no a no a no a no

IN WHICH I TRY BIRDS

Storm petrels move
me to a college in the desert.
Great egrets keep me here
so I never have to see
him, his hands
gripping the remote control, thigh
of the couch.

By the sound of low tide,
I could send a night heron
into his throat, enter
his massive belly
for missing frogs, lacewing,
crawdads. We would leave nothing
unturned there. Momma,
I'm making all As. I'm never
coming home.

TEETH OF OUR HOUSE

The foyer seems small
with Momma there.
I don't know how her body got
like that.

It must have taken
flight, shoulders as wings, lifting
up the stairs & back down again.

She must have cracked
like the deer in the car door: sudden,
face-first
into an object unknown to her.

We have two hall tables. We have ceramic
lamps & three sets of keys.

If I am right & women are winged deer,
would they still chew grass,
mouth mulberries under
a porch light?

She sips tea like nothing
happened, never tells anyone.
Nothing happened. We never lived
in a house with stairs.

I DESIRE A DREAM I DESIRE

The moon is our invitation to want.
Our ruined want. Ecstatic want.
Holy want. Endangering
want. What we want we will
eager into existence. A language
of wants. Who wants to undo,
open, oppose the shutter.

They crawl on top of you,
& you think this is it.
They a lowering cloud.
The bus runs all on its own.
The driver faces us. Their back
is trusting the technology
of roads & gates. We pass
through doors & doors
in a loud clang. To anticipate
the crash is to hold your body
in reason, each muscle
a preparation. Our spines,
the mission of movement,
faster. The bus accelerates
when it knows to.
We are scared in our knowing.
There are more doors to pass.

The moon is never in this dream.
Never in the sex dream or escape
dream. The moon never hovers
in a car dream. We rarely look up.
One time I looked up in a dream,

& there were endless
stars cozy in their familiar black.
One time I looked up in a dream
& saw a great metal technology
working in the sky. Little desert
memory oblique. The stormbirds
flit from curse to curse.

IT IS IMPOSSIBLE TO ATTEMPT

whatever it means to back again   undo

renascent makes me think: revolutionary lavender

one way of being born is without a mother
back to original place   where is
who is   home

whose familiar vanilla or pine candle inter   rogates
       both our ribs to touch   always woods surround my home

don't you fucking bring that word into this house

anew   once more   to turn   vascular
      back   through the oaks

what does it mean to control your own body to con-
tort your own sweetness   into sugar thrown acorn

if I lower my body into the dirt the clay
       will the juniper the fern the log
require shade   grow public like one becoming   *Girl*

the number of us   is practically infinite

IF I WANT TO CUM

I have to quiet
the prey in me
who say run
run kick run
back to the sweet
girl before queer
recognized the body
recognized a type
of violence of grief
shame on me
for wanting
ecstasy
is a religion of men
& my gender can no
longer pray
at the entrance
of empty cups

I am not asking
for a drop
I am asking
for a few minutes
so that I might
twist my history
right on out my body
set it on the nightstand
see myself in blushing
light & want
to be their lover too

TRANS US THE NEW GODS

a leaf borrows the tree / the air machine steals / the show wakes the whole audience /
I am here / on the days you are here / where can we go if not together

ii.

the snake its tail hooks rock
at water's edge the water
knows the boundaries
snake knows the possibility
in reach

ii.

I am hiding my fist
all the time I pass
from rage to rage to rage
I pass you on the way

ii.

I can see the top of the house is attics & eyes
an occupant breathing

ii.

I hate the way prayer feels submissive
I'd rather come to god
sidereal like a new colleague with the same degree

ii.

what we suffer aching out our finger
steeples I cut the sky up &
upward
that cloud is a donkey
that cloud is a bitch
I know I know   if we lose
the spectacle it's just sawdust &
air / but what about the trees / their hands / the saw whirring & whirring & worrying
into the center memory / our sky opens / imagine the spill of us

ACKNOWLEDGMENTS

My gratitude to the editors of the following journals & magazines in which some of these poems have appeared, sometimes in different versions.

AZCentral Poetry Spot: "Teeth of Our House"
Blue Earth Review: "Some Fish" & "Ode to Flathead Catfish" &
  "How to Measure Pain from the Top of an Oak Tree"
Boulevard: "Tongues" & "Church"
ELKE "A Little Journal": "Alternative to Burying"
ELM: "When There Is No Evidence upon Initial Assessment, We
  Must Re-Examine the Body" & "Men Can't See Me" &
  "Transfiguring the Dinner Table"
Heavy Feather Review: "Witch Hunt"
Juked: "House Fire"
The Ocean State Review: "Choose a Password: Childhood Nickname"
Poetry South: "In the Wild"
Threadcount: "Taking to Water"

I am over the moon with gratitude. This book is a dream made true by the support of so many folks.

Endless gratitude to Carl Phillips for seeing the possibility in my book & to the editors of Autumn House Press, Christine Stroud & Mike Good, for guiding it into the world with such care.

Thank you to the teachers & fellow writers & community from Guilford Technical Community College, University of North Carolina at Greensboro & Arizona State University. Thank you to John Gillikin at GTCC for your encouragement & introducing me to the MFA. Thank you to Stuart Dischelle & Rebecca Black for your support & guidance at UNCG. Thank you to my ASU committee, Norman Dubie & Cynthia Hogue, for your dedication to my work. All my love & gratitude to Norman Dubie who taught me to embrace the strangeness of memory & imagination, who held the mirror so I could see myself as a teacher. You are missed beyond language. To Sally Ball & Natalie Diaz for your guidance through & beyond the MFA. To Natalie Diaz, whose workshop opened me toward imagining the foundational images of this book. To my MFA peers & cohort at ASU for your support & invitations to wonder. Your attention helped nourish the first drafts of some of these poems.

My love to María Alvarez, Aria Curtis, Michael Holladay & Charlee Moseley. Thank you for your friendship. For holding space for me & loving me. Let's have a bbq workshop soon.

Thank you to the folks at Queer Poetry Salon, tanner menard & Julián Delacruz, for creating a space where queer writing can live. Reading at the open mic surrounded by community back when it was held in a living room in Tempe was a necessary moment toward believing in myself.

Immense gratitude to TC Tolbert & the workshop writers of Trans/Space is Expanding—my first queer writing home. Your vulnerability & bravery inspired & nourished me. Here I learned to "show up for the nothing." Y'all expanded my imagination toward possibility & supported me so that I might conceive of this book. Thank you.

Thank you to C.T. Salazar, a poet who helped me see that the Queer South has always been alive & I was never truly alone there. Thank you for your time & care with my poems.

To the writers & thinkers who imagined with me, inspired me, challenged me, workshopped with me, invited me to read or publish, or supported drafts of these poems along the way: Jada Renée Allen, Imogen Arate, Lauren Berry, Dexter Booth, Molly McCully Brown, Marci Calabretta Cancio-Bello, CA Conrad, Meg Day, Julián Delacruz, Hop, Dana Levin, Che Che Luna, Josh Rathkamp, Rashaad Thomas, Elijah Tubbs & Vanessa Angélica Villarreal.

Thank you to my family who let this weird fish swim. To my Grandpa Bob for initiating me into a family of Irish storytellers & face-makers. To my parents for all the times you nourished me as a writer. Thank you to my momma for helping me learn my voice. Thank you to my dad for loving my strange imagination. Y'all are both oral storytellers of different traditions & have influenced the storyteller in me.

Thank you to my beloved, my partner, my water, Michael Pérez. You have loved me beyond. I live & this book lives with gratitude for you, your boundless love.

NEW AND FORTHCOMING FROM AUTUMN HOUSE PRESS

Discordant by Richard Hamilton
Winner of the 2022 CAAPP Book Prize, selected by Evie Shockley

The Neorealist in Winter: Stories by Salvatore Pane
Winner of the 2022 Autumn House Fiction Prize, selected by Venita Blackburn

Otherwise: Essays by Julie Marie Wade
Winner of the 2022 Autumn House Nonfiction Prize, selected by Lia Purpura

Murmur by Cameron Barnett

Ghost Man on Second by Erica Reid
Winner of the 2023 Donald Justice Poetry Prize, selected by Mark Jarman

Half-Lives by Lynn Schmeidler
Winner of the 2023 Rising Writer Prize in Fiction, selected by Matt Bell

Nest of Matches by Amie Whittemore

For our full catalog please visit autumnhouse.org.